THE
Archive Photographs
SERIES

GREAT YARMOUTH

The mineral water firm of H. Lawrence & Son loading up early one morning in 1902 ready for the day's deliveries. The picture was taken in Hammond Road looking towards Northgate Street. The building on the right was used to manufacture Ginger Beer, Soda Water and Lemonade from 1896 until the mid 1970s. It is now part of Newtown Motors. The postman on the left did not intend to be left out as he posed for a moment while delivering to Moat Place. Mr Lawrence stands proudly in front of his workforce.

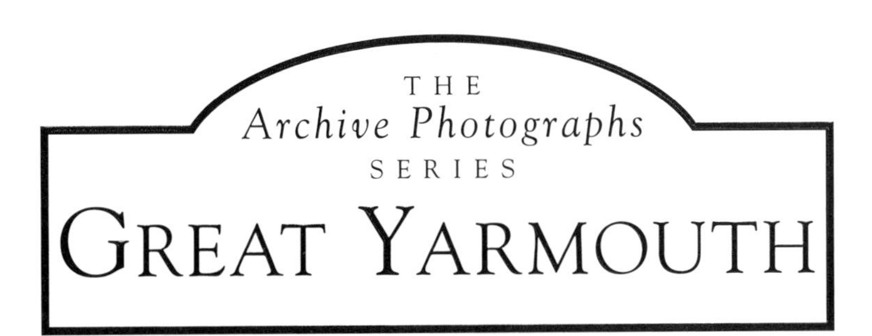

Compiled by
Colin Tooke

First published 1995

The Chalford Publishing Company
St Mary's Mill, Chalford,
Stroud, Gloucestershire, GL6 8NX

ISBN 0 7524 0329 X

Typesetting and origination by
The Chalford Publishing Company
Printed in Great Britain by
Redwood Books, Trowbridge

To Jan

Contents

The penny omnibus, here crossing Haven Bridge, first appeared in the town in March 1897. The company had ten vehicles painted red and yellow and seventy horses, This one is on the Southtown Station to Jetty route. Other routes were Vauxhall Station to the Aquarium and Newtown to Friars Lane. The company had a short life, being superseded by the electric tram car in 1902. Note the London steamer berthed at the Hall Quay in the background.

Introduction

The street scenes, buildings and daily life of the people who lived in Great Yarmouth and Gorleston have been recorded by the camera from the days of the pioneering mid-nineteenth-century photographers right up to the present day. The advent of the picture postcard, towards the end of the last century, added to this pictorial record of the past. During the hey-day of the picture postcard in the first decade of this century, millions of cards were sent by holidaymakers and visitors to every corner of the country, mostly promoting the sea-side aspects of the town.

The pictures in this book, most of which have not before appeared in print, have been arranged in sections to cover a wide cross-section of town life including industry and commerce, leisure and pastimes, people and places. Together with the captions, the photographs in each section provide a potted history of a particular subject. The early history of the town has been recorded in print many times before but this book doesn't attempt to repeat that, instead it is an illustrated account of some selected aspects of the last hundred years, from the 1870s to the 1970s, and hopefully, it will appeal to both the serious historian and to the casual browser. Pictures of the fishing industry will bring back many nostalgic memories for local people as too will those of trams, buildings, work places, and some of the social events that are recorded here. The largest upheaval to the town in recent years was the re-alignment and virtual destruction of Fullers Hill, the carving of Temple Road through the centre of the town and the construction of the Market Gates shopping centre, all of which took place in the early 1970s. Parts of the town, familiar to generations of its inhabitants, were destroyed in a few months, but fortunately some of these changes were recorded by the camera and can now be included in this book.

It has been impossible to include all aspects of the old town in this one book but hopefully there will be an opportunity at another time to continue this pictorial history in a further book of this kind.

Charles Dickens, the great nineteenth-century author, wrote his thinly disguised autobiography, *David Copperfield*, after a brief visit to Yarmouth. In the book one of his characters is quoted as saying ' ... upon the whole, Yarmouth is the finest place in the universe'. One hopes this was also Dickens's personal view of the town and perhaps after reading this book you will agree with him.

Colin Tooke
1995

Tramcar No. 24 at the Gorleston Beach terminus in 1905. The early morning paper boy has paused to get in the picture. The only advertisement on the tram is for McGowan the gentleman's outfitters in Regent Street, Great Yarmouth, a shop which later became Grimwades.

One

Travel and Transport

From the horse-drawn bus to the modern motor vehicle, Great Yarmouth and Gorleston have enjoyed a large variety of public transport systems over the years. Horse-trams only ran in Gorleston and the technical problems of crossing the Haven bridge with tramlines meant that an integrated transport system between Yarmouth and Gorleston had to await the introduction of motor buses in the 1920s. With the improvements in transport, visitors to the town in the summer months found the horse brakes replaced by charabancs allowing for excursions further afield and opening up new areas of countryside including the Broads area. When the motor car appeared, garages sprang up to sell and maintain the new marvel of the age. With the introduction of vehicle licensing the town was allocated the unique prefix EX which identified public and private vehicles for many years. The following pages illustrate the changing methods of travel and transport in the town.

A horse tram at Feathers Plain in January 1897. The Gorleston horse-tram service began on 25 March 1875 and ran from Southtown Station to Feathers Plain. The line was later extended to Brush Quay via Lowestoft Road and England's Lane.

Extra horsepower was required at certain points on the route and here a 'trace' horse has been added to assist the tram car on the incline at the junction of England's Lane and Lowestoft Road in May 1897. The extra horse was also used in winter when ice made the going slippery.

The Gorleston horse-trams were replaced by electric-trams on 4 July 1905. This is the first tram being driven on that day by the mayor, Alderman Mayo, turning into Baker Street.

The same section of track as in the picture above being taken up after the Gorleston tram service finished on 25 September 1930.

An electric-tram on the sea front in 1902. The service began in Yarmouth on 19 June 1902. In the background is one of the last horse-buses and behind that a horse-brake passing the Bath Hotel.

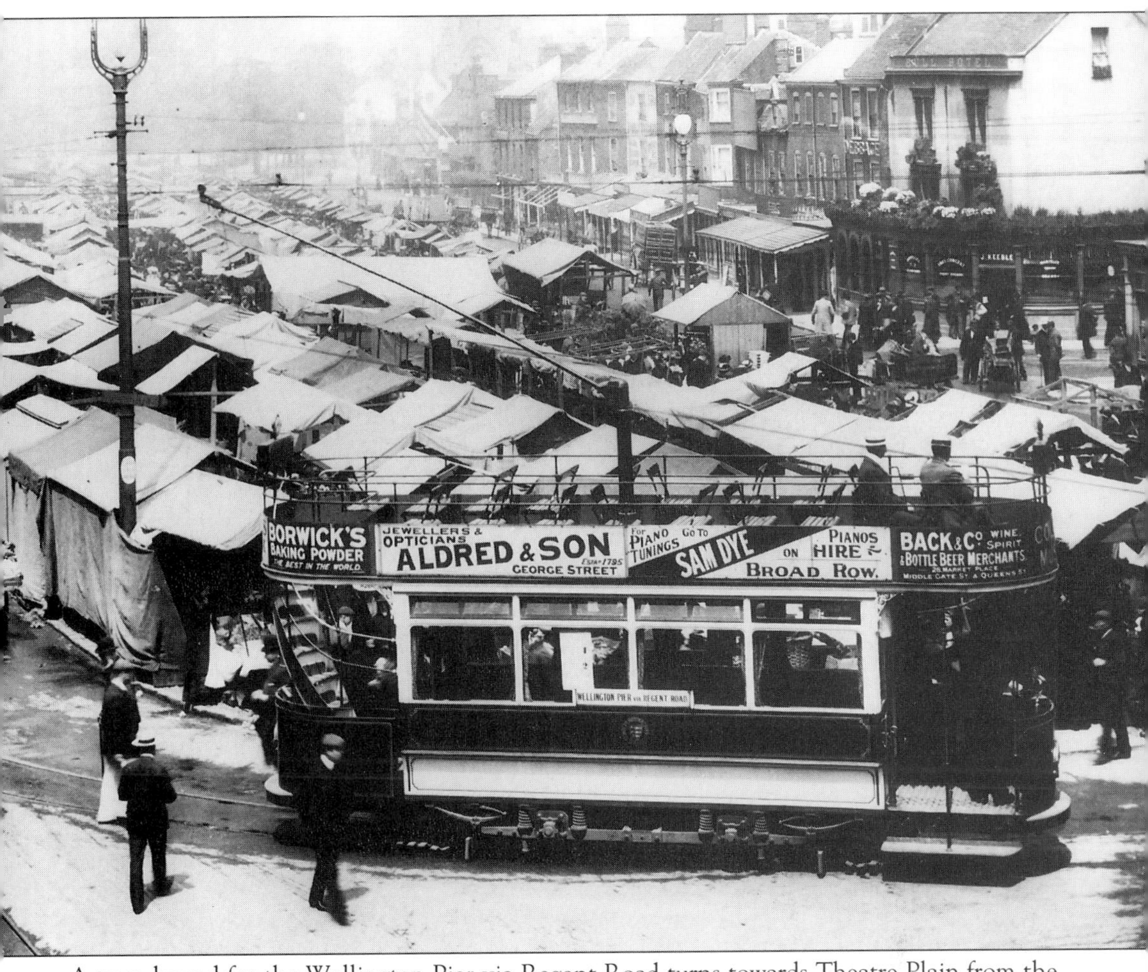

A tram bound for the Wellington Pier via Regent Road turns towards Theatre Plain from the Market Place in 1904. The livery of the trams was maroon and cream. In the background is the Bull Hotel on the corner of Market Gates which closed in 1911 and later became the corn store of Arthur Hollis. Note the seats on the open top deck of the tram with movable back rests which could be altered depending on the direction the tram was travelling in.

Opposite: The top of Regent Road in August 1902. Two horse-buses are passing each other while in the background is one of the new electric-trams which spelt the end for the horse-drawn transport. Each horse-bus used three pairs of horses each working day. The sandwich board men on the right are advertising a play *A Message From Mars* at the Theatre Royal.

The last major extension of the Yarmouth tramway system was the route to Caister. This was the first tram on that route on 16 May 1907 seen here at the Caister terminus with the Green Gate public house in the background. The mayor and members of the transport committee stand proudly in front of the tram. Behind the tram and just visible to the right of the picture is a horse-drawn tower wagon, ready in case of accident to the overhead wires.

Redundant tram car bodies being towed away from the Gorleston depot along Church Lane by a traction engine in 1931. Many of these old trams were taken to Caister Holiday Camp. Trying to pass the trams is one of the new omnibuses which had replaced them.

One of a fleet of five large fifty six-seater buses delivered to the town in 1928 to replace some of the trams. This one, on the sea front, is on the Newtown to Pleasure Beach route. These buses were all commandeered by the Army in 1940.

St Johns garage, Regent Road, on the day of opening 11 May 1911, with a fine display of early motor vehicles.

Two taxis ready for a wedding in Crown Road in the 1920s. Note the long white coats worn by the drivers.

A charabanc ready to leave Theatre Plain for a Sunday School outing to Herringfleet on 17 June 1924. It was the custom to give charabancs a name and this one has *Princess Mary* painted on the bonnet.

Popular with holiday makers in the 1920s were charabanc trips from the sea front. This one is advertising a trip to California Cliffs returning via Winterton lighthouse and the Broads for four shillings (20p).

One of the early single deck buses belonging to the United Automobile Services, forerunners of the Eastern Counties Co., about 1930.

One of three buses bought from the London General Omnibus Co. in 1925. The buses retained their London red livery and were disposed of early in 1928. Each bus cost £125 plus £176 to cover the cost of an overhaul.

Barrels of Lacons Yarmouth Ale being delivered by a Claydon Steam Wagon early this century. The brewery used a variety of transport methods including a fleet of trollcarts in the nineteenth century. Horse-drawn drays were used until 1920 when a fleet of motor lorries replaced them. In 1936 the company owned 171 pubs in Yarmouth.

A milk delivery barrow in the 1920s. The Worlingham Dairy was at 156, Nelson Road Central until the 1950s.

A funeral *c.* 1910, shortly after the introduction of the motor hearse. The funeral director is Mr Henry Brundish, seen here with his son David. The firm of Brundish & Son was established in 1893 with premises in Bermondsey Place.

Two

Public Houses

'There is nothing which has yet been contrived by man by which so much happiness is produced as by a good tavern or inn', said Samuel Johnson in the eighteenth century. Towards the end of the last century the total number of public houses, from the large coaching inns to the small beer-houses in the town, approached 300, the greatest concentration being along the quays and around the market. There were few restrictions on opening hours although in 1872 drinking time was cut to seventeen hours a day, opening time being 6am until 11pm. The oldest pub in Gt Yarmouth is undoubtedly The Feathers in Market Gates, the original of which was selling ale before 1581, a time when 32 gallons could be bought for three shillings and fourpence (16p). The local brewery, Lacons, which, before the last war owned 120 public houses in the town, has now gone. Over the years many public house names have changed, and such changes are still going on. The pubs illustrated in this section have been chosen to give examples of all types in the town, some large, some small.

The first (or last) public house on South Quay, appropriately named the 'First and Last', was just inside the south gate of the old town wall. In 1772 it was called the Dolphin and later the Ship on the Stocks as it was nearly opposite a shipbuilding yard. The building was demolished in 1989 and the site is now a car sales yard.

On the south side of Nelson's Monument was the Nelson Hotel, well-known for its large open-air Skittle Alley. In 1920 a new hotel was built to the east and named the Nelson. The old house was used from 1945 as office accommodation for the nearby Erie Resistor factory.

The Clarence Tavern was on the corner of Clarence Road and Havelock Road. The building to the left had formed the southern entrance to the Victoria Pleasure Gardens which closed in August 1872 and the site was redeveloped for housing. Clarence Road and other nearby roads were all swept away in the redevelopment of the area in the 1970s.

The Anchor and Hope was on the corner of St Peter's Road and St George's Road. On the extreme right can be seen the Hippodrome Circus building. The pub closed in 1935 and was demolished, the site becoming a Dodg'em Track and in the 1960s the Circus Zoo. Today it is a gift shop.

The Recruiting Sergeant is still a public house on the corner of Alma Road and Trinity Place. Seen here in June 1905 when Frederick Crane was a beer retailer and also ran a general store. The poster on the wall is for the Royal Aquarium advertising a musical comedy, *A Trip to Chinatown*, which ran for the week commencing 26 June 1905.

Until 1940, No. 93, Havelock Road was a small beer house with the pretentious name of Crystal Palace. Small beer houses such as this did not have spirit licenses. At the end of the last century the landlady was Mary Ann Hall, a milk seller as well as a beer retailer. Modern housing now stands on this part of Havelock Road.

On the corner of Nelson Road and Albion Road stands the Great Eastern, which in the 1880s was known as the Hearty Tar. The date on this advertising postcard is 1912. Fordham's Ales were brewed in the small Hertfordshire village of Ashwell and this was the only public house in the town to sell their beers.

The Britannia, at 46, and 47, South Market Road, was one of the public houses owned by the Corporation and leased to Lacons. The landlady, Mrs Mary Tooke, is seen here on the left in this photograph from 1917. It closed in August 1941 and is now a cafe.

The Rose in King Street closed in 1910. In 1822 it was described as 'a porter shop, frequented by rough customers from Yarmouth beach'. A Lacons house it was sold to Divers & Son in 1904. The Rose had an entrance in Theatre Plain as well as King Street. Today it is the site of H. Samuel's jewellery shop.

The Marine, on Marine Parade, was originally known as the Admiral Onslow and Nelson's sailors are said to have drunk here. In 1819 it became a Lacons house and the name changed to the Marine Tavern in the 1820s when John Denny was landlord. It then became the headquarters of the Denny Company of Salvagers, one of the seven salvage companies on Yarmouth beach. In the forecourt can be seen the oyster stall of J. Symonds. This picture was taken *c.* 1920.

The Duke's Head on Hall Quay in 1945. One of the town's finest examples of Jacobean architecture, this was originally a merchant's house built in 1609. From here the London stage coach set out in the seventeenth century and it is thought that it was this inn that Charles Dickens had in mind when writing his book *David Copperfield*. He described David setting out for London by stage coach from the yard of an inn. On the left is Henry's Café, better known locally as the Greasy Spoon.

The original Crown on the corner of Regent Street and King Street became a public house in 1834. It was demolished in 1881 and the building seen here erected. In 1966 it closed and was demolished the following year when Dewhurst butchers was built on the corner. The shop is now a bakery.

Opposite: Fish Stall House in the Market Place in March 1971, a few months before it closed. In 1972 it was demolished to make way for the new Market Gates development. In the eighteenth century it was called the Jolly Butchers and in 1883 was changed to the Market Tavern. Nichol's Restaurant on the right was a popular lunch time rendezvous for local and market people.

An outing about to depart from the Earl Beaconsfield on North Denes Road early this century. The four-horse-brake was the forerunner of the charabanc. The pub is named after Benjamin Disraeli, the statesman and friend of Queen Victoria who was created first Earl of Beaconsfield in 1876.

The White Swan on North Quay belonged to Paget's brewery in 1819 and later to Steward & Patteson. In 1953 the Highway Committee recommended the demolition of the White Swan to improve traffic flow along the Quay.

The Saracens Head on the corner of Church Plain is now the insurance office of J. Critoph. Originally known as the Cart and Horse this pub closed in 1970.

The East and West Flegg, Northgate Street was on the corner of Row 2. Earlier known as the Bird in Hand and in 1822 the Black Horse it finally closed in 1925. Carrier's carts to the villages of Caister, Ormesby and Rollesby left here at 4pm every Saturday. The site is now a disused property on the corner of Rampart Road.

The old Kings Arms in Northgate Street in September 1880. Fixed to the wall can be seen a steelyard, an ancient weighing device used to weigh carts before the introduction of the weighbridge. This was one of only three inns in Norfolk to have such a fixture.

ESTABLISHED 1772.

BURROUGHS,

FAMILY

WINE & SPIRIT MERCHANT

Direct Importer and Bonder.

WHOLESALE AND RETAIL STORES:

1 & 2, MARKET PLACE;

Bonded Stores: No. 15, Row 20; and No. 8, South Quay.

A large variety of well-matured WINES and SPIRITS always in Stock, at the Lowest Prices compatible with first-class quality and strength.

	Per Bottle.		Per Gallon.	
Fine Old BRANDIES, Pale or Brown	4/-	4/6	24/-	27/-
Fine Old WHISKIES, Irish or Scotch	2/9	3/6	16/-	21/-
Burroughs' Choice Old Jamaica RUM	2/4	2/10	14/-	16/-
Anderson's Celebrated Old Tom GIN	2/-	2/4	11/6	13/-

Ports from 24/- per doz. Sherries from 20/- per doz.

WHOLESALE BOTTLER AND AGENT FOR

Bass', Allsopps', Guinness's, and Lacons' Beers.

☞ SEE PRICE LIST.

ALL ORDERS RECEIVE IMMEDIATE ATTENTION. DELIVERIES DAILY.

An 1894 advertisement for Burroughs. Three years later this wine and spirit merchant was bought by Lacons. The property was destroyed by bombing in 1942 and now the Gallon Pot stands on the site unable, however, to sell brandy for 20p a bottle.

The Waggon and Horses was on the corner of Garrison Walk, now Garrison Road, and Northgate Street (then called Caister Road). In 1819 it was owned by Paget's brewery and later Lacons. Carriers left here for the villages of Thurne, Winterton and Stokesby. The pub closed in August 1905.

Opposite: The Cromwell Temperance Hotel was established in 1890, extending a two-storey building (see above). When the old Star closed the licence was transferred to the Cromwell which then became the new Star. The old Star was demolished in 1935 when the adjacent telephone exchange was extended.

The old Star Hotel had been a tavern since *c.* 1789 and closed in September 1930. Seen here in the 1880s with the 'station fly' outside, the coach which met the trains and carried customers to the hotel. The building on the left was later to become the present day Star Hotel (see below).

The Steward & Patteson site on North Quay earlier this century. Havenbridge House now stands on this riverside site from where S. & P. beers were distributed to over one hundred outlets in the Yarmouth and Lowestoft area. The company wherry *Annie* brought two loads each week in winter, three in summer, from the brewery in Norwich. The delivery horses were replaced by lorries in 1945. The depot closed in 1969 and was demolished in the following year. On the right is the Cellar House public house owned by S. & P., which closed in 1939. In the nineteenth century this had been the Watermans Arms.

Three

The Fishing Industry

'Of all the fish that live in the sea, the herring is the King.' Great Yarmouth was was once the largest herring port in the world. The 1913 fishery was the most prosperous ever known. At Yarmouth 823,600 crans (one cran equals approximately 1320 fish) were landed and sold at an average price of 20 shillings (£1) per cran. Over 1000 boats fished from the port. The majority of the catch was exported to Russia and Germany but after 1918 these export markets did not revive and the North Sea quickly became over-fished as other European countries developed their own fishing industries. The last drifters fished from the port in 1970, the great herring fishery had finished and an industry associated with the town since its foundation, almost a thousand years earlier, had gone for ever. An integral part of the Yarmouth fishing season was the Scots fisher girls who travelled south with the fleet to gut, salt and pack the herring. Each girl could gut over 60 fish a minute, working a day that began at 6am and continued until the last catch of the day was done, sometimes late into the evening.

A Yarmouth trollcart outside the salt store of Norford Suffling near the Fishwharf. in the 1880s. These carts, specially designed to negotiate the narrow Rows of the town, were first used in the sixteenth century and were also known as 'Harry Carries'. Before the construction of the Fishwharf in 1869 fish was landed near the Jetty and transported into the town's curing houses by carts such as this which were about twelve feet long and just over three feet wide. With their low back axle and wheels under the body they were very easy to load.

Steam paddle tug *Reaper*, owned by Nicholson's Towage Co., towing a group of local smacks out of harbour *c.* 1900. The centre boat (YH 1052) is the *Primrose*, built in 1882 for W. Stanley of Southtown. The *Reaper* was sunk in a collision off Gorleston Pier in 1901.

The *Meteor*, owned by the Star Tug Co., towing Scottish fishing boats, known as Zulus, into harbour. This tug was built on the Tyne in 1857 and broken up in December 1911.

The drifter *East Holme* (YH 22) leads a group back to port *c.* 1930 watched by onlookers on the old Gorleston Pier. This drifter was built in 1912 and broken up following a collision in 1934.

Scots girls chat with a crew member of a drifter. Boats from Fraserburgh (FR), Yarmouth (YH), Buckie (BCK) and Inverness (INS) can be seen among others moored at the Fishwharf in the 1930s.

The steam drifter *Morning Star* (YH 479) was built in 1907 and owned by J. More. The crew of a drifter usually consisted of the skipper, mate, hawseman, net stower, two deckhands (or Yonkers), engineer, fireman and cook.

'Swills' of herring waiting to be taken to the curing yards or packed for export *c.* 1910. The drifter on the left, *Thirty* (YH 695), was one of the Smith's Dock Trust fleet which all had numerical names. *Thirty* was launched in 1902 and eventualy broken up in 1935. In 1915 the boat was taken for naval service in common with many other drifters.

A view from the Nelson Monument with the old power station chimney in the background and showing a small part of the hundreds of thousands of barrels required each year for the fishing industry.

A boat from the small Scottish community of Buckie unloading fish into 'swills'. These baskets were unique to the Yarmouth fishing industry and each one held about 500 herring.

Motor transport slowly replaced horse power along the quays. These early lorries are bringing barrels of herring to be loaded for export to many European countries c. 1910.

Steam drifters moored at the Fishwharf in 1956. The brick chimney is part of the old electricity generating station and beside that is the chimney of the gasworks. Bloomfield's Ocean House can be seen to the right of the picture.

Barrels of salted herring waiting to be loaded for export in the 1930s. Note the coal trucks waiting to refuel the drifters. Although the Russian market had been greatly reduced after 1918 there was still a large Scandinavian market.

Two Scots girls take a break from their work. Their bandaged fingers can clearly be seen. These workers followed the herring's seasonal cycle, beginning at Shields in the spring and finishing in East Anglia in the autumn. They were as much a part of the fishing scene as the drifters.

Scots girls usually worked in teams of three, two gutting, one packing. One team could deal with about 3000 fish in an hour. The fish were sprinkled with salt otherwise they would be too slippery to handle at speed. This was a cold as well as a messy job.

Off duty the girls could usually be seen in the town engaged in animated conversation with each other, knitting quickly as they walked. Because of the strong fish odour their lodging rooms were often cleared of furniture except for the bed and a wooden box or trunk.

A group of Scots fisher girls salting and packing the gutted fish into barrels ready for export. Regardless of their age they were always referred to as 'girls'. In 1913 there were 6000 of these girls in the town for the autumn fishing season.

The Prince of Wales paid a visit to the fishing industry on 21 October 1930. He is in the centre of the picture surrounded by fisher girls and fishermen.

These girls are waving to the Prince of Wales during his tour of the Fishwharf. On the same day the royal visitor had opened the new Haven bridge.

At Gorleston there were many curing yards along Riverside Road. The fish were tipped into these wooden troughs called 'farlanes' ready for the girls to gut. This postcard is dated 1913.

Each fishing boat carried about one hundred nets, each net about thirty-five yards in length, these would be joined together to make a continuous length of almost two miles. The men seen here are 'ransackers' whose job it was to check the nets for damage.

The coffee tavern and grocery store of Robert Redgrave on the Fishwharf c. 1910. On the right is a salt store belonging to the Great Yarmouth Fish Selling Co. Ltd.

The first steps towards mechanisation were taken in 1929 when Bloomfield's installed herring boning machines. In the 1950s the firm installed gutting machines as seen here at their Ocean House premises on South Denes Road.

Four

Celebrities and Ceremonies

As was the custom in the late nineteenth century and the first part of this century the town marked special occasions, such as Royal accessions or jubilees, with public announcements from the site of the old market cross in the Market Place. The town's streets were decked with bunting and flags for visiting dignitaries, conferences and national events, the townsfolk taking every opportunity to celebrate and enjoy themselves. The first carnival was held in 1923 followed by others in 1924 and 1934, providing a week of fun and entertainment. These were ambitious events, comprising historical pageants, sporting events, competitions and processions involving thousands of people. From Royal celebrations to seaside beauty contests, this section illustrates just a few of the many special events that have taken place in the town in years gone by.

Roasting a bullock at Brush Quay, Gorleston, as part of the Diamond Jubilee celebrations on 22 June 1897. Colonel Combe, deputy Mayor, (a maltster who lived at Ferryside) has the carving knife and is closely watched by the Revd Forbes Phillips (Vicar of Gorleston 1893-1917), wearing a top hat.

Celebrations for the Diamond Jubilee of Queen Victoria in Yarmouth Market Place in 1897. The shops in the background have now been replaced by the Co-op store and Argos.

The Church Congress procession on 1 October 1907 in the Market Place, returning from St Nicholas church. The Archbishop of Canterbury and over forty bishops attended the congress which lasted for four days.

The official proclamation of the accession of King George V being read by the Town Clerk on the site of the old market cross on 9 May 1910. In the background is Market Gates with the Bull hotel on the left. In the centre background, on the corner of Fish Street is the stove warehouse of Cooper & Cunningham, forerunners of the present day Coopers.

A peaceful march by the local branch of the Suffragettes, passing over Haven Bridge *c.* 1912.

Admiral Beatty in the town on 20 June 1919 to receive the Freedom of the Borough and seen here passing along a decorated Regent Street. Admiral Beatty had commanded the fleet at the Battle of Jutland in 1916 and became an Admiral at the age of 39.

The first motor vehicle to travel the Acle New Road without paying a toll on Wednesday 10 March 1920, carrying the Mayor Mr W. Bayfield. The toll for a motor car had been sixpence ($2\frac{1}{2}$p). The tollgate is on the right, held open by a policeman. Although still referred to as 'new' the road was opened in 1832.

The 1923 Carnival was held from 30 June to 7 July. Outside the new bathing pool are, left to right: Mr and Mrs Middleton (Mayor and Mayoress), King Carnival, Louis Rump and Mr and Mrs Brett (Deputy Mayor and Mayoress). Louis Rump later became the town's Publicity Manager.

Saturday 30 June 1923. One of the highlights of the Carnival was a re-enactment of Nelson landing at the Jetty. This pageant included 200 characters with Mr Earnest Tunbridge taking the part of Nelson and sailors and marines from HMS *Garry* and HMS *Kennett*.

Wednesday 4 July 1934. A pageant on the Lower Parade, Gorleston, as part of the Carnival. Over 1,300 people took part in this pageant called 'The Mountbanks'.

A float in the Carnival on 3 July 1934 entered by the Herring Industry Board. After the Carnival this float toured many towns and cities in the country to promote the herring industry.

Wednesday 4 July 1934. The Carnival procession at Gorleston where John Bull greets King Carnival (Mr Backhouse Archer) on Brush Quay. On the right is Miss Yarmouth, Rose Addy.

Monday 2 July 1934. A re-enactment of the visit of Richard II to Yarmouth in 1382 was staged on Church Plain as part of the Carnival. King Richard was played by Alan Tunbridge and his Queen by Molly Boning.

The Yarmouth Bloaters speedway team of 1950. Left to right: Bill Carruthers, Billy Bales, Bert Rawlinson, Tip Mills, Reg Morgan (seated on bike), Johnny White, Fred Brand, Wally Higgs. Speedway began at the Caister Road Stadium in 1948 and in 1950 the team was promoted to Division II of the National League. Later in the 1950s speedway gave way to Stock Car racing.

The decorations along Marine Parade to celebrate the 1953 Coronation.

Local girl Miss Patricia Sewell (now Mrs Patricia Severn) being crowned by Ken Dodd as winner of the 1959 Battle of Britain beauty contest at the Marina. On the right is Neville Bishop whose band first played at the Marina in 1938. Ken Dodd played the summer season at the Britannia Theatre.

Five

Railways

The mid-nineteenth-century railway explosion reached Yarmouth in 1844 when the first railway in Norfolk opened on 1 May to connect the town with Norwich. Southtown station opened in 1859 and Beach in 1877. Gorleston was brought into the rail network in 1903 following the construction of the Breydon rail bridge. Passenger traffic increased as the holiday trade developed, reaching a peak in the 1950s. In 1958, on each summer Saturday, forty express trains originated in the town, sixteen from Vauxhall, twelve from Southtown, eight from Beach and four from Gorleston. The port, industry and the fishing were all catered for by a quayside tramway from Vauxhall along North and South Quays to a terminus at the Fishwharf. Following the demise of the fishing industry this line was used for container traffic and in 1962 carried 24,500 containers of frozen food from Birds Eye and pulp products from Hartman Fibre. Yarmouth shared the decline of the railway network with the rest of the country. Beach station closed in 1959, Southtown in 1970 and the quay tramway in 1975. Today only Vauxhall remains to connect the town with the national rail network and all goods traffic has now been consigned to the roads.

An engine at Southtown Station in the 1870s. Standing beside the polished engine is the stationmaster.

A steam train approaching Southtown station in 1953. The station had been closed from 31 January to 18 February that year by the East Coast floods. A signalman was stranded in his box for twenty one hours before being rescued by boat. Sandbags are still piled either side of the line when this picture was taken.

A steam train and a diesel unit at Southtown in 1958. An important summer service from Southtown in the 1950s was the 'Easterling' express which left London at 11.03am each morning and arrived at Yarmouth at 1.38pm, stopping only at Beccles.

Southtown station in 1959. The station closed 2 May 1970 and was then used by the Santa Fé Oil Co. as offices until it was demolished in 1977 to make way for Pasteur Road.

A Great Eastern train at Vauxhall in 1904. Trains such as this carried the large Bass outings to Yarmouth from Burton-on-Trent. In 1897 the June outing brought 9000 people on fifteen special trains, running at ten minute intervals, to the town. The last Bass outing to Yarmouth was in 1913.

Vauxhall station yard in the 1920s and a tram waits to take passengers into the town. In the foreground the tram tracks can be seen passing over the railway bridge, erected in 1847, which is now only used for pedestrian access to the station.

A steam train approaching the platform at Vauxhall in August 1958. Two car diesel units started working from Vauxhall in 1955. In the background is the M. & G.N. over bridge carrying the line from Beach to the Breydon Bridge.

Vauxhall station concourse in 1933. The W.H. Smith bookstall can be seen in the background. The platforms were extended in 1959 to take twelve coach summer specials, diverted from the closed Beach station. The station buildings were rebuilt in 1961.

Railway police at Yarmouth Beach station in 1912.

Beach station July 1958. There were three platforms at Beach as well as a loco depot and turntable. The last train from this station ran on 28 February 1959 and the track was removed within a few weeks. A coach station now stands on the site.

A Drewry 204 hp diesel locomotive leaving Vauxhall for the Quay tramway in August 1958. Note the side skirt and cow-catcher, a requirement for trains working a street tramway system. Each train was proceeded by a railwayman carrying a red flag as it made its slow progress along the Quay.

Traffic is brought to a halt on Hall Quay as a train of Birds Eye containers makes its way along the Quay in the late 1950s. Note the coal trucks in the siding near the bridge. Cars parked close to or on the line made the journey a slow one. On North Quay the line served Lacons Brewery, a sawmill and Wenn's Box factory while on South Quay the line fanned into four tracks where cranes were available for ship or rail freight transfer. The terminus was at the Fishwharf where there were long sidings with loading bays.

A steam shovel excavating the cutting during the construction of Gorleston station in 1901. The line opened on 13 July 1903 and was built by the Norfolk & Suffolk Joint Railway. Today this is part of the Gorleston by-pass.

A steam train leaving Gorleston station bound for Yarmouth Southtown in the 1950s. Gorleston station was in a cutting, the ticket office being at Victoria Road level. A footbridge linked the up and down platforms.

Gorleston North station was damaged in a 1941 air raid and closed the following year. Passengers reached this station by a slope from the north side of Burgh Road.

Breydon Swing bridge opened in 1901. There were four spans to carry the M.& G.N. line over Breydon water almost on the same line as the modern by-pass road bridge. The bridge closed in 1953 and was demolished in July 1962. In the top right of the picture is the Vauxhall station engine shed and turntable, now the Asda supermarket site.

Six
The Town Centre

The Market Place formed the centre of the medieval town. From here all trade could be conducted and people kept informed of national events by the town crier, and the townspeople could celebrate special occasions. For hundreds of years the Market Cross formed the centrepiece but the last one on Yarmouth market was demolished in 1836, the site is, however, marked by a stone plaque. The Market Place was larger than today, extending to the town wall where butchers and fishmongers had their own sections to trade from. Market days would see the country folk bring their produce into town to sell, at first from baskets and later small stalls. A few still carry on this trade but increasingly the market caters for fancy goods and hardware. The medieval trade fairs changed to pleasure fairs in the late seventeenth century and this tradition is still carried on in the week following Easter. The area has always changed to meet the changing needs of the people and now, although pedestrianisation has arrived, the Market Place with its surrounding shops still forms the heart of the town.

Market day *c.* 1930. The corn store of Arthur Hollis can be seen on the corner of Market Gates and the church has its pre-war spire.

George Sill, Ironmonger, at number 23 Market Place in 1925 just before the shop closed down. On the left is Row 40 and the wall of the Central Cinema, both of which are now part of Woolworth's store. Note the Golden Key trade sign above the shop. This shop is now JJB Sports.

The Market Place as it looked throughout the 1970s. Traffic flows in a clockwise direction around the market in the days before pedestrianisation..

The Easter Fair in 1910. Note the dress of the boys as they gather around the ice-cream barrow. The first Yarmouth Fair was held in April 1684.

Thurston's Great Show at the 1909 Easter Fair. The dancing girls are in front of the 120-key Marenghi Organ. It was at fairground shows such as this that moving pictures were first shown, several years before the days of the cinema.

The shop of A.S. Cooper at 32, Market Place in 1898. In 1975 the shop became Norfolk Radio and is now Hughes TV. On the left is Row 49.

Ernest Carpenter outside his tobacconist shop at 26, Market Place c. 1900. Row 44 can be seen on the left and on the right the dining rooms of Mrs Palmer which later became Smith & Daniels. In more recent years number 26 was the Army & Navy Stores and is now the Heart Foundation charity shop.

Seen here in 1925 are, from right to left: Smith & Daniels, Carpenters (see page 75), the Angel Hotel and Backs. The Angel was demolished in 1957 and by 1973 the these shops were occupied by Radio Rentals, Army & Navy Stores, Bellmans Wool shop, International Stores and Heneky Inns. Today the shops are Radio Rentals, Heart Foundation, Leeds Building Society, Dixons and the Card Company. Note the sign for the Central Cinema on the lamp post (see page 72).

Opposite: Numbers 1 & 2 Market Gates *c.* 1900 when bloaters were 1/- (5p) a box. Part of the old Fish Market, these shops later became Carr's Newsagents and then Stricklands and were demolished as part of the Market Gates development.

A shop window display by Fieldings, 35, and 36, Market Row, in the late 1950s when Mobo toys were all the rage. The equivelant price for the 54/11 cycle in decimal coinage would be £2.75.

June 1974 showing the extent of the town centre demolition required for the new Market Gates shopping complex under construction. Buildings not yet demolished are the Electric House in the foreground and the Printing Works in Theatre Plain. (see page 79). The road line for Temple Road has not yet been cleared from Priory Plain.

(Opposite, bottom) The Printing Company works, Theatre Plain, in 1906. This later became the printing works of John Buckle. The building, built in 1899, also housed the Conservative Club and Botwrights, gentlemens' hairdressers, seen on the left with Fish Street running through to Market Gates, demolished in 1974 (see page 78).

Part of the medieval town wall exposed by demolition of Cooper's property in Market Gates, seen here in March 1974. This section of the wall has now been preserved and runs through the centre of the shopping complex.

Albert Kerridge, King Street *c.* 1920. The shop was rebuilt in 1950 and taken over by Brahams in 1957. Later it became the Gas Showroom until that closed at the end of 1994.

The interior of Kerridge's drapers and hosiery shop which was established in 1886. Note the chairs for customers. This was before the days of 'self-service'.

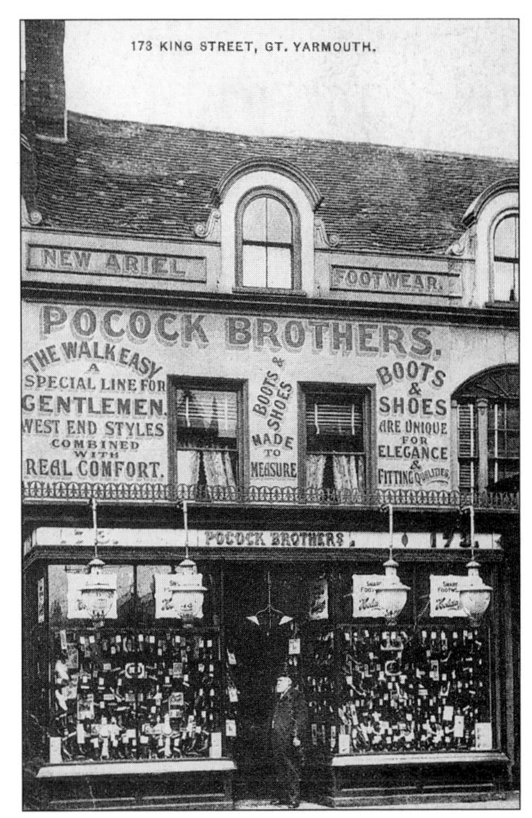

Pocock Brothers shoe shop was taken over by Freeman, Hardy and Willis in 1910. On the left is Row 74, taken into the Central Arcade when it was built in 1926. Today the site, which has been a shoe shop for over 120 years, is on the northern corner of the Victoria Arcade and is called Shoe Express.

Hedge's shoe shop on the corner of King Street *c.* 1908. This is now Burtons. The shop with the sunblinds in King Street is Bonings (see page 82). On the right is Arnold's store which was destroyed by fire in 1919.

King Street 1905. In 1910, Livingstones was Smith & Daniels and Browns had become the Domestic Bazaar. The large shop next door, between Rows 64 and 65, was Boning Brothers (see below).

The shop front of Bonings c. 1900. The firm sold out to Marks & Spencer in May 1932 who still trade on the same site today. When Marks & Spencer opened here nothing in the shop cost more than 5/- (25p). The building was rebuilt following war damage.

In 1874 this was a college for young ladies. In 1886 it was a carpet and furniture shop owned by W. Bartram who later sold it to George Carr. Early this century the shop was taken over by Skippings who still trade from this fine building.

'Ye Music Shoppe' of Arthur Watts in 1908. In 1910 number 15, and 16, King Street became Wolsey & Wolsey and remained so until the 1940s when it became Turner's shoe shop. On the first floor is White's Teeth Institute advertising a complete set of teeth for one guinea or a single tooth for 2/6 (25p). Note the unusual trade sign of a double bass and two banjos over the shop.

The western end of Regent Street with Beezor's Old Furniture & China store on the corner. This was bought in 1912 by the Post Office and the following year a new post office was built on this prime corner site.

Prisoners being put into a horse-drawn Black Maria, outside the Middlegate police station in 1889, following a court appearance. The Town Hall can be seen on the right.

Endersby's furniture shop, 5 and 6 Church Plain, next door to the Wrestlers Inn *c.* 1910.

By the 1930s David Yerrell, the auctioneer, was at 5 and 6 Church Plain. The Wrestlers Inn is on the right and just visible beside it is the chemist shop of Thomas Woodcock on the corner of Howard Street. These shops were destroyed in an air raid in 1943, the Wrestlers was rebuilt after the war.

Fullers Hill in the 1890s. On the right is the Crystal and in the background is the Albion Tavern, a public house which closed in 1912 and was a private house for several years.

Fullers Hill in the 1960s. To the right of Cubitt's fish shop is the motor cycle shop of Clarke and Knights. All these buildings were demolished in 1970 when Fullers Hill was widened in conjunction with the new river bridge. Only the Crystal remains.

Cobb's Place off Middle Market Road in 1906. The cart on the right belongs to Hunts, the mineral water firm who had stables here and a factory in Howard Street.

Seven

Trade and Industry

Although the fishing industry formed the backbone of the town's growth and prosperity for hundreds of years, shipbuilding and marine engineering also flourished in the busy seaport town, as did numerous trades associated with fishing, such as barrel and box making, net and sail making and the more ancient crafts of ropemaking and cork cutting. Manufacturing industry came to the town in the early nineteenth century when Grouts began silk production. Following the Second World War the South Denes area of the town saw the development of larger industries. Erie Resistors electronics factory, Birds Eye Foods and Hartman Fibre began to develop land that had traditionally been reserved for the rapidly declining fishing industry. Many smaller industries have come and gone in the town that are too numerous to mention. Today the oil industry dominates the riverside area and new smaller industries have taken over from the large, mass employers of the past.

The area around Nelson's Monument in 1947. Near the Monument can be seen the original Nelson Hotel and to the south the Millora works of Erie Resistor. On the river side of this are the beginnings of the Bird's Eye complex which, with Erie, was soon to take over much of the land seen in this photograph. The two storage tanks to the right were oil tanks built to refuel naval vessels in the port during the war; these were demolished in 1948.

The town's first power station was built in 1894. Coal was brought from the quay in small horse-drawn trucks and later by overhead conveyor. The station stopped producing electricity in 1959 and the chimney was demolished in 1961.

The South Denes power station under construction in 1956. This station was opened in September 1958.

The Yarmouth Gas Company was formed in 1824 and the works on South Denes Road continued to make coal gas until 1965. The Retort House, seen here in 1956, was demolished in 1968.

The interior of Crabtree's marine engineers on Southtown Road. The firm was established in 1854 and was renowned for its marine engines.

A Lowestoft trawler on the slipway at Richards, Southtown Road in the 1970s, the last shipyard on the river. Before 1970 this was Fellows yard.

A nineteenth-century shipyard with the Yarmouth ship *William Henry* under construction. Wooden boats such as these, limited to 500 tons because of the width of the river, were built at many shipyards along the river bank. In 1818 nearly one hundred vessels were built along the river Yare.

Norfolk Lines Atlas Wharf in 1983 with the *Duchess of Holland* loading trailers. The terminal, established in 1969, expanded to take in part of the old Fish Wharf and gasworks site. The last ferry operated by Norfolk Line from Great Yarmouth left port on 31 January 1992 after which the company moved to Felixstowe.

The first Ro-Ro ferry, the *Duke of Holland*, was brought into service by Norfolk Line in January 1969. The original white livery was changed to black in 1974 and blue in 1986. Two of the deck trailers have the Dutch spelling of the company name 'Lijn' which was then known as the Norfolk Ferry Service.

Before the well-known Norfolk Line trailers came into use the company ran trials with this type of unitised cargo, transferred from Superior International ships to lorry by crane.

The Caister Road factory of Smith's Crisps opened in March 1935 and continued production until 1982. The factory was demolished in 1986.

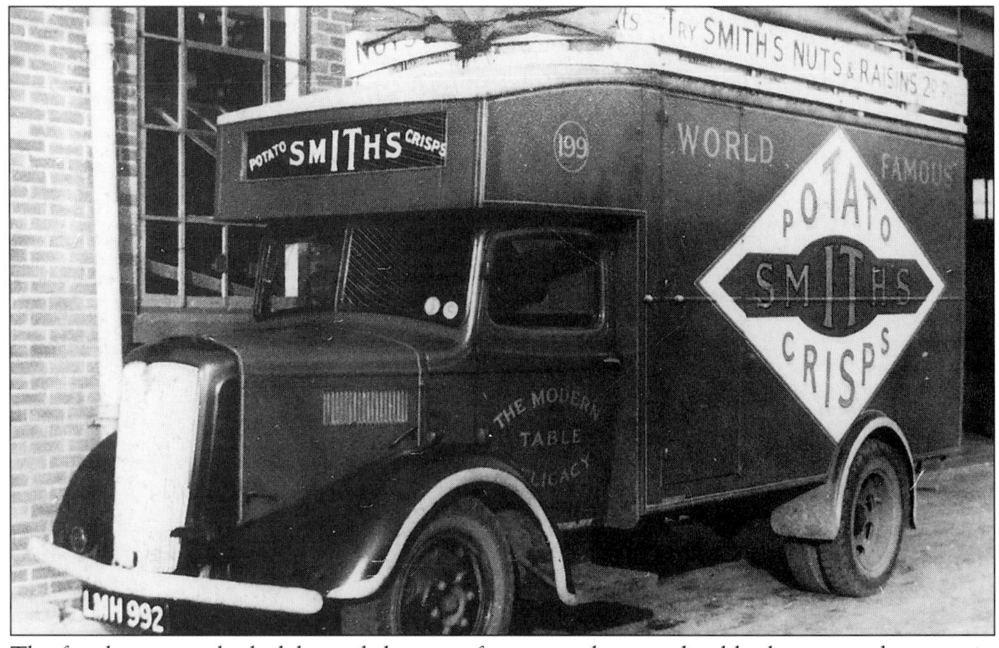

The familiar vans which delivered the tins of crisps to shops and public houses in the town in the 1950s and 1960s. The roof rack was used for empty tins.

The last working mill in the town was this postmill on Hamilton Road which stopped grinding corn in 1906. Known as Greengrass Black Mill it was built in 1851 on what would now be the corner of Hamilton Road and Windsor Avenue.

Press's High Mill at Southtown was built in 1812 and was claimed to be the highest mill in England The four pairs of stones could grind thirty cwt of oats per hour. It was demolished in 1904.

A cornmill at Cliff Hill Gorleston known as Beevor's mill. It was demolished in 1887.

The workers at the Great Yarmouth Printing Company in Theatre Plain, photographed in 1903 (see also page 79).

Grout's silk factory was established on this site in 1815 and is seen here in 1957. The factory entrance leads from St Nicholas Road at the bottom of the picture and on the far right is the Garibaldi Hotel. The public house beside the factory gate was the Factory Tavern, now called the Tudor Tavern. The houses to the west comprised Belfort Place. Sainsbury's supermarket and car park now occupy the site of the factory and Belfort Place.

The Long Room weaving shed early this century. These looms wove the black silk mourning crepe for which Grouts was famous throughout the Victorian period. Note the complete lack of safety guards on the machinery.

Workers leaving Grouts factory gate in 1904. At this time the factory employed about 1400 people. The straw hats everyone seems to be wearing were very fashionable in the Edwardian age.

A rare picture of block printing on silk *c.* 1908. In the background can be seen the finished silk scarves.

The factory in the 1950s. This machine carried out the final process of measuring and rolling the fabric prior to dispatch. The factory closed on this site in September 1972.

Eight
Along the Prom

Generations of holidaymakers have enjoyed themselves at the resorts of Great Yarmouth and Gorleston. The present day holiday industry was founded in the mid-nineteenth century when the introduction of the railways, combined with new Bank Holidays, gave the working man an opportunity to get away from the drudgery of the industrialised towns. A week at the seaside became fashionable and by the turn of the century resorts around the coast were flourishing. A range of entertainments quickly developed from early beach concert parties. New pavilions and theatres were opened and the sea front promenade became the focal point of the town for the summer months. The 1950s were the halcyon days of the modern British seaside holiday but as foreign travel came within the reach of more people the seaside declined in popularity. This section shows some of the developments along the promenade in the first half of this century, a development trying to keep pace with the ever increasing demands of the holidaymaker.

The Revolving Tower. Built in 1897 to the north of Britannia Pier the tower was 120 feet high. The cage, holding 150 people, revolved as it went up and down the tower. There were only five such towers in the country. The Yarmouth one was demolished in 1941.

These young ladies are enjoying themselves on the sands near the Revolving Tower early this century.

The Britannia Refreshment Saloon on the south side of the pier in the summer of 1921. Note the beach photographer's camera on the left.

The Gravity Switchback Railway opened in 1887. It was sited on land to the east of the new Wellesley Recreation Ground but in 1900 was moved to the north of Sandown Road. The ride closed at the end of the 1909 season.

Henry Binke's electric railway started on 27 July 1885 on the beach near Britannia Pier. It ran for less than two weeks, the rails being taken up on 10 August 1885, the company having been declared bankrupt.

A beach service in 1903. Note the lady with the harmonium on the left.

Another familiar scene on the beach in 1903 was the Phrenologist who would tell a person's fortune by the shape of their head. Seen here is Professor Durham operating near the Jetty. Another site near the Britannia was run by a local lady known as Madame Cook.

The Britannia Pier in August 1921. The pavilion seen here was the third to be built on the pier which has suffered from several fires and disasters since it was first built in 1858.

One of the first disasters to beset the Britannia Pier was on 28 November 1868 when the *Seagull* of Kings Lynn was driven through the pier during a storm.

The Britannia Pier's third pavilion. The ballroom and the Long Bar were all destroyed by fire on 20 April 1954.

The Jetty shelters, 16 August 1902. The canon in front of the kiosk is one of a pair of Russian guns brought to the town in 1857. They stood near the Jetty until 1941. The lookout belonged to one of the many beach companies that operated a salvage and lifesaving service from the Yarmouth beach. Note the smartly dressed Edwardian holidaymakers.

A four-horse-brake sets out from the Jetty taking holidaymakers on a trip to the countryside, while others climb the lookout. In the foreground is a horse-drawn tea stall.

Goat carriages took children for rides along the seafront until 1911. From then licenses were only issued for ponies. The covers would indicate that this is a wet summer's day without many customers, probably in the 1870s.

The Jetty Dining Rooms in 1900 when they were run by the Garrett brothers. They were previously known as Palmer's Cocoa Rooms. After being badly damaged by fire they were rebuilt as an amusement arcade, now called the Golden Nugget.

This advertisement for the dining rooms indicates the prices holidaymakers paid for their food in 1900 with a dinner costing 1/- (5p) and fish and chips 2p.

The lifeboat house, on the corner of Standard Road is now disguised as Ghost Blasters. The first lifeboat was stationed at Yarmouth in 1825 and until 1883 there were two boats. The station closed in 1919. Here the boat is being manhandled across the parade to the beach.

The Yarmouth lifeboat *John Burch* was on station from 1892 until 1912 and was built by the local boatbuilders, Beeching Brothers for £227.

The Sailors Home (now the Maritime Museum) was opened in 1859. On the roadway are a line of goat carriages and in the background is Papworth's Mill in York Road, demolished in 1881.

The Bathing Pool opened on 22 July 1922, seen here shortly after that date. In the background, to the right of the Sailors Home, is the Royal Alfred Hotel and to the left the Jetty Dining Rooms (see page 112) now belonging to Ellis.

Laying the new tram tracks along the Parade and into St Peters Road in the winter of 1902. On the corner of St Peters Road and St George's Road can be seen the Anchor and Hope public house.

Foulsham's Bath Hotel is now the Flamingo amusement arcade. This was the site of the first Bath House where people could, from the mid-eighteenth century, bathe in sea water for medicinal purposes. The foundations of the seaside resort as we know it today were laid in this period.

This building was part of the Bath Hotel. Bought by George Gilbert in 1903 it was demolished in order that the new Hippodrome Circus could be seen from the Parade. This open forecourt remained until the 1970s when amusements were built on it.

Gilbert's first circus, in this wooden building, opened 25 July 1898. In 1902 the new Hippodrome was erected on the same site.

The Hippodrome Circus and forecourt in 1910. The Tally-Ho water spectacle ran from 1 August to 24 September that year and was seen by 120,000 people.

George Gilbert, founder of the Yarmouth Hippodrome circus, and his wife, Jennie O'Brian, performing at a circus in Paris in the 1880s. An accident ended his career as an equestrian.

The Marina and car park in 1952, now the site of the Marina Centre. At the end of the Britannia pier can be seen the Ocean Ballroom which burnt down in 1954. In the centre of the picture is a 'Dr Who type' police telephone box.

The Guinness Clock, standing in front of the fountain near the Marina, in 1954. Originally made for the 1951 Festival of Britain these clocks toured seaside resorts throughout the 1950s.

The charabanc park and putting course between the bathing pool and the Jetty in the late 1920s. Afternoon trips to Brundall Gardens are advertised for 5/- (25p) and evening trips to Sea Palling for 3/- (15p). The putting course is today the Arnold Palmer crazy golf course

The Royal Hotel was the first seaside hotel to be built in the town and opened in 1840. Charles Dickens stayed there for a few days in 1848. The hotel is seen here before it was partly rebuilt in 1877.

This version of Peggotty's Hut stood on the beach opposite the Empire cinema from 1928 until 1933. Run by J. McKenzie Aylott, it contained about one hundred paintings and thirty statuette characters from *David Copperfield*.

Among the oldest buildings on the Parade are these cottages on the corner of Waterloo Road. A date stone on one reads, East Anglia Place 1837. The corner cottage is now a gift shop and the other, the Las Palmas restaurant. The ornamental woodwork above the windows still exists.

The bandstand in the Wellington Pier south garden in July 1934. Military bands played afternoon and evening in the gardens which were opened in 1900. On Bank Holiday Sunday 2 August 1914 over 12,000 people visited the gardens.

In June and July 1928 this band, the Queen's Bays 2nd Dragoon Guards, played in the Wellington Pier Gardens twice daily. The last appearance of a regimental band in the bandstand was on 26 August 1939.

Dancing in the Winter Gardens in the 1950s. The 1965 season was the last time dancing was held here during the summer months.

Roller skating in the Wellington Pier gardens in the 1950s. Skating started in the Winter Garden in 1907 and in the outside gardens in 1908. In the 1930s football on skates was very popular.

Pixieland opened 5 June 1954 on what was the south lawn of the Wellington Pier Gardens. In 1956 it was renamed Caveland and closed after the 1957 season.

The present day Model Village opened on 20 May 1961 on the old Pixieland site.

Shadingfield Lodge was originally built as a summer villa in 1865. It remained a private house until 1952 when Lacons bought it and converted it into a public house.

An interior view of Shadingfield Lodge in the 1880s. The Prince of Wales stayed here several times between 1872 and 1897.

Gorleston c. 1900. The Cliff Hotel was built in 1898 on the cliffs overlooking the harbour. It burnt down in 1915. In the centre is the Pavilion and to the right the Pier Hotel. Gorleston developed as a quieter holiday alternative to its neighbour Great Yarmouth. The Parade was extended in 1903, shelters built and the Ravine cut through the cliffs.

The Gorleston Pavilion opened 30 July 1900 and was the Corporation's first effort to enter the field of indoor entertainment. Elsie and Doris Waters were among the well-known entertainers to appear at the Pavilion before the last war.

The Gorleston swimming pool, demolished in 1994 after much controversy, was a popular place in the 1930s, as it was on the day that this photograph was taken.

Acknowledgements

Four photographs in this book are taken from a public collection, the remainder are from private ones painstakingly put together over many years. One such collection, which has formed the nucleus of this book, is that of the late Ted Goate (1909-1993), local historian and an authority on theatre history. Without this outstanding collection the book would not have materialised and, therefore, I hope this volume will be a small memorial to Ted, who was a friend for many years.

I am indebted to Charles Read ARPS whose superb photography of the town in the 1950s has also made a valuable contribution to the book. Other material has been provided by Gordon Berry, Charles Lewis (former curator of the Maritime Museum), John McBride and Alec McEwen, to all of whom I am most grateful.

For her patience and help in choosing the photographs and continued encouragement, I thank Jan, without whom the book may never have seen completion. Only she knows the difficulties we have overcome.